Handwriting

Book 4

Sue Peet

William Collins' dream of knowledge for all began with the publication of his first book in 1819. A self-educated mill worker, he not only enriched millions of lives, but also founded a flourishing publishing house. Today, staying true to this spirit, Collins books are packed with inspiration, innovation and practical expertise. They place you at the centre of a world of possibility and give you exactly what you need to explore it.

Collins. Freedom to teach.

Published by Collins
An imprint of HarperCollinsPublishers
77–85 Fulham Palace Road
Hammersmith
London
W6 8JB

Browse the complete Collins
Education catalogue at
www.collinseducation.com

Previously published as *Spectrum Handwriting* by Folens Ltd, first published 2000.

10 9 8 7 6 5 4 3 2 1
ISBN: 978-0-00-742705-5

British Library Cataloguing in Publication Data
A Catalogue record for this publication is available from the British Library.

Acknowledgements
Fonts from *Handwriting for Windows* used with the permission of KBER.
The author and publisher wish to thank the following for permission to use copyright material:
Laura Cecil Literary Agency for the poem `The Intruder' by James Reeves from Complete Poems for Children, FaberFinds copyright © James Reeves. Reprinted by permission of the James Reeves Estate. Anthology available at www.faber.co.uk/faberfinds; and The Society of Authors for the poem `Cargoes' by John Masefield, reproduced by permission of The Society of Authors as the Literary Representatives of the Estate of John Masefield.
Every effort has been made to trace copyright holders and to obtain their permission for the use of copyright material. The author and publisher will gladly receive any information enabling them to rectify any error or omission in subsequent editions.

Design: Mark Walker
Illustrations: Chantal Kees
Cover design: LCD
Cover illustration: Gwyneth Williamson

Printed and bound by Martins the Printers, Berwick-upon-Tweed.

Contents

Programme overview

Book	Age	Main Content	Main Teaching Aims	Primary National Strategy	Cambridge International Primary Programme
A	Age 4–5 Nursery/Reception/P1 Foundation stage	Pencil control Hand-eye coordination Movements necessary to form letters	To make controlled pencil movements To join two points with a straight or curved line To follow a given sequence of movements	Use a pencil and hold it effectively to form recognisable letters, most of which are correctly formed	
B	Age 4–5 Reception/P1	Pencil control Letter-like movements Recognition of lower case letters linked to upper case letters Upper case letters (alphabetical order) Numbers 0–9	To produce a comfortable pencil grip To produce a controlled line that supports letter formation To write upper case letters using the correct sequence of movements To recognise lower case letters	Use a pencil and hold it effectively to form recognisable letters, most of which are correctly formed	
1A	Age 5–6 Year 1/P2 (Term 1)	Precursive lower case letters, grouped according to movement Recognition of lower case joins Upper and lower case links	To develop a comfortable and efficient pencil grip for forming and linking letters To recognise upper and lower case counterparts To form lower case letters correctly in a script that will be easy to join	Write most letters, correctly formed and orientated, using a comfortable and efficient pencil grip	Develop a comfortable and efficient pencil grip Form letters correctly
1B	Age 5–6 Year 1/P2 (Terms 2 and 3)	Lower case letter formation and joins in a cursive style using common rime patterns Main punctuation marks	To reinforce the link between handwriting, spelling and the recognition of phonic patterns and letter strings To practise correct letter orientation, formation and proportion	Write most letters, correctly formed and orientated, using a comfortable and efficient pencil grip Write with spaces between words accurately	Develop a comfortable and efficient pencil grip Form letters correctly
2	Age 6–7 Year 2/P3	High-frequency word practice Print in the environment Letter joins through common spelling patterns and strings Print for labels, notices etc. School and classroom vocabulary Beginnings of self-assessment	Practice in basic sight vocabulary Reinforcement and practice using the four basic handwriting diagonal and horizontal joins Linking handwriting to phonic and spelling knowledge and patterns Conceptual awareness of space required for printing (for labels, notices etc.)	Write legibly, using upper and lower case letters appropriately within words, and observing correct spacing within and between words Form and use the four basic handwriting joins	Form letters correctly and consistently Practise handwriting patterns and the joining of letters

Scottish Curriculum for Excellence
First stage, Writing (Tools for writing): I can present my writing in a way that will make it legible and attractive for my reader (LIT 1-24a)

National Curriculum for Wales
Foundation Stage objective: develop a legible style of handwriting in order to follow the conventions of written English and Welsh

Revised Northern Ireland Curriculum
Key Stage 1 objective: use a legible style of handwriting

4

Book	Age	Main Content	Main Teaching Aims	Primary National Strategy	Cambridge International Primary Programme
3	Age 7–8 Year 3/P4	Reinforcement and practice of print and cursive style Copy writing Uses to which handwriting may be put High-frequency word practice Development of spelling patterns	Reinforcement and practice of cursive and printed style to ensure consistency in size and proportion of letters and the spacing between letters and words Purposes and uses of handwriting and print	Write with consistency in the size and proportion of letters and spacing within and between words, using the correct formation of handwriting joins	Ensure consistency in the size and proportion of letters and the spacing of words Practise joining letters in handwriting Build up handwriting speed, fluency and legibility
4	Age 8–9 Year 4/P5	Copy writing Uses to which handwriting may be put High-frequency word practice Development of spelling patterns Development of a personal style Speed writing practice	Reinforcement and practice of cursive and printed style to ensure consistency in size and proportion of letters and the spacing between letters and words Purposes and uses of handwriting and print Consolidation and development of a style that is fast, fluent and legible Presentation, layout and decoration of 'finished' work	Write consistently with neat, legible and joined handwriting	Use joined-up handwriting in all writing
5	Age 9–10 Year 5/P6	Copy writing Development of a personal style Speed writing practice Uses to which handwriting may be put	Purposes and uses of handwriting and print Consolidation and development of a style that is fast, fluent and legible Presentation, layout and decoration of 'finished' work	Adapt handwriting for specific purposes, for example printing, use of italics	Review, revise and edit writing in order to improve it, using IT as appropriate
6	Age 10–11 Year 6/P7	Copy writing Development of a personal style Speed writing practice Uses to which handwriting may be put Links into ICT and fonts	Purposes and uses of handwriting and print Consolidation and development of a style that is fast, fluent and legible Presentation, layout and decoration of 'finished' work	Use different styles of handwriting for different purposes with a range of media, developing a consistent and personal legible style Select from a wide range of ICT programs to present text effectively and communicate information and ideas	Use different genres as models for writing Use IT effectively to prepare and present writing for publication

Scottish Curriculum for Excellence
Second stage, Writing (Tools for writing): I consider the impact that layout and presentation will have and can combine lettering, graphics and other features to engage my reader (LIT 2-24a)

National Curriculum for Wales
Key Stage 2 objective: present writing appropriately (develop legible handwriting; using appropriate features of layout and presentation, including ICT)

Revised Northern Ireland Curriculum
Key Stage 2 objective: develop a swift and legible style of handwriting

Teacher notes

General introduction

Collins Primary Focus: Handwriting is a comprehensive programme designed to support teachers and children through the stages of learning a clear, fluent, legible and fast style of joined writing from the early stages to the top of the Primary phase. The programme provides copiable material that is intended for use through shared sessions, guided group tuition and individual practice.

The programme begins with patterns and movements, which will be necessary to improve hand-eye coordination, fine motor control and individual letter production.

Linked to National Curriculum levels and the Primary National Strategy, the programme encourages a precursive and then a cursive style from the early stages of learning.

The programme aims to link the development of handwriting skills and style to the main patterns and rules of the English spelling system. As children practise the movements necessary to make the joins and patterns of the handwriting scheme, they are also reinforcing the patterns of the main onset, rime and spelling patterns.

By Book 2, children are provided with an opportunity to experiment with alternative letter shapes when forming their own personal handwriting style.

Books 3–6 introduce the notion of keeping a handwriting folder containing samples of material that will prove useful when presenting and setting out work for publication. The books include many uses to which both printing and joined handwriting skills may be put.

Books 3–6 also introduce the concept of two types of handwriting: one style may be used for 'speed' tasks, e.g. personal note-taking; the other, neater, style may be used for presentational work. Self-assessment sheets are included in Book 3 (pp.20 and 63) and Book 6 (p.20). Books 3–6 also link handwriting skills to the basic skills of layout and presentation on a computer keyboard.

The joining of letters in words: which style is most appropriate?

Teachers will always have views about the efficacy or attractiveness of specific letterforms.

It must be remembered that every adult will consider the formation that they use to be the most comfortable to them. However, this does not necessarily make it the most effective formation for children learning for the first time. Teachers must bear in mind the need to develop a handwriting style that is clear, fluent, legible and fast for children learning for the first time.

What about exceptions?

For children with dyspraxia or other handwriting difficulties, the teacher may need to look for SEN support. These children may already be receiving handwriting tuition as part of their support.

Children who move schools may well have already learned another handwriting style. If they enter school during the Infant stage, teachers may wish them to recap pages from the previous book, and this may be completed – with the cooperation of parents – as a homework activity. Children who move schools during the Junior stage may well have formed a personal handwriting style, which, although different, is clear, fluent and legible. It may be inappropriate to alter their handwriting style at this stage.

The notes on particular handwriting difficulties (see p.14 of the Teacher notes in Books 1A–2) may also provide useful information.

Letterforms in the programme

Collins Primary Focus: Handwriting aims for the development of joined handwriting as soon as individual precursive letterforms have been mastered. Specific letterforms have been selected to meet the following criteria:

● They should help children's handwriting to be clear, fluent, legible and fast.

● Each individual lower case letter chosen begins from the main writing line.

● Each lower case letter is taught with both a lead-in and a lead-out stroke. This is to help avoid confusion in young children about whether to begin a letter at the top or the bottom. It has also proved to be beneficial for children with poor hand control and for dyslexic children.

- The joined lower case letters should, where possible, resemble closely their printed counterparts.
- Letters, such as 's' should have the same form wherever they occur in a word, thus reducing the amount that children need to relearn.
- It is possible to join all lower case letters. One letter ('f') changes from the precursive to the cursive stage. While it is felt that the 'f' used in Book B will be familiar to young children learning to form the precursive letters, the cursive 'f' is used from Book 1A to encourage a more fluent hand.
- The pencil or pen should need to be lifted from the page as little as possible when linking lower case letters in words, thus reinforcing the patterning of joined movements within letter strings as an aid to memorising phonic and spelling patterns.

Precursive Upright (Book B)

A B C D E F G H I J K L M
N O P Q R S T U V W X Y Z
a b c d e f g h i j k l m
n o p q r s t u v w x y z
The quick brown fox jumps over the lazy dog.

Cursive Upright (Books 1A–1B)

A B C D E F G H I J K L M
N O P Q R S T U V W X Y Z
a b c d e f g h i j k l m
n o p q r s t u v w x y z
The quick brown fox jumps over the lazy dog.

Cursive Slanted (Books 2–6)

A B C D E F G H I J K L M
N O P Q R S T U V W X Y Z
a b c d e f g h i j k l m
n o p q r s t u v w x y z
The quick brown fox jumps over the lazy dog.

The following letter styles have been chosen to meet the preceding list of criteria:

Specific letter style options

The reasoning behind each cursive letter style option chosen for use in *Collins Primary Focus: Handwriting* was discussed with several Literacy and SpLD (Dyslexic) practitioners who agreed with the choices.

f	Chosen because, looped from the back, it is easiest to link to all other letters, always joining the same way and thus more fluent.
s	Chosen because it joins in the same way whether it is at the beginning, in the middle or at the end of a word, thus making it fluent and meaning there is less for children to learn.
v	Chosen because it is more legible, most like the printed 'v' and less likely to be confused with the letter 'u'.
w	Chosen because it is more legible, most like the printed 'w' and less likely to be confused with the letter 'u'.
x	This is the only small letter that requires the pencil/pen to be lifted from the paper. This style was chosen because it will join and because it is most like its precursive counterpart. A curved 'x' can often be confused for the letters 'sc'; this is particularly so for dyslexic and less able readers.
y	Chosen because it is more legible, most like the printed 'y' and doesn't involve taking the pencil/pen off the paper.
z	Chosen because it will join and because it is most like its precursive counterpart.

As children move on to join letters in words, they will learn that many letters will join in different places, depending on the letter they are linked to. The programme aims to support the development of strong links between the formation of patterns in handwriting and those involved in phonic and spelling knowledge.

Contents of the programme

Infant Stage

Book A: Foundation Stage and Reception/P1

This book introduces the fine motor movements and pencil control that will be necessary for the formation of letters and patterns. It provides practice in moving from left to right, keeping within 'tramlines' and making the up-and-down and curved movements necessary for letter formation.

Book B: Reception/P1

This book reinforces movements and patterns that will help children to make the movements they will need when learning to form letter shapes. For many children the movements from left to right and from top to bottom may not be intuitive, hence the instruction to 'Start at the ☆.'

Practice is also provided in each of the movements for upper case letters. These have been placed early in the programme because many children will have learned at least some of these letters before they begin formal schooling, and so any inappropriate movements can be corrected early.

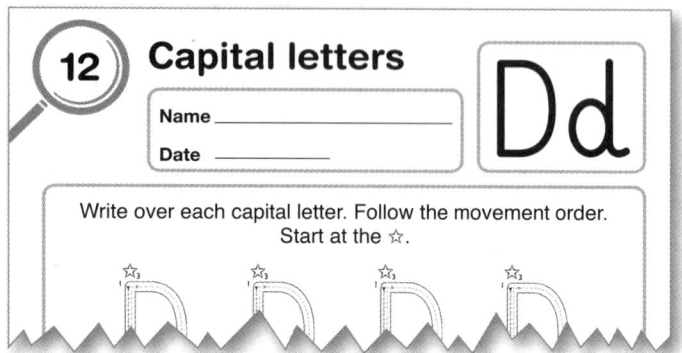

Book 1A: Year 1/P2 (Term 1)

Linked closely to the National Curriculum and Primary National Strategy, this book provides more intense teaching strategies and practice for the first term of formal tuition.

Since it is at this stage that children may learn incorrect or inappropriate movements, each individual letter shape and movement is taught with a lead-in and a lead-out stroke beginning from the writing line. The letters are grouped according to the main movements involved so that children gain extra reinforcement of the shapes and movements involved. By grouping letters according to their movement, it is also hoped to avoid the confusion that many children encounter between letters that may look very similar in print, e.g. 'b' and 'd', 'p' and 'q', 'n' and 'h'.

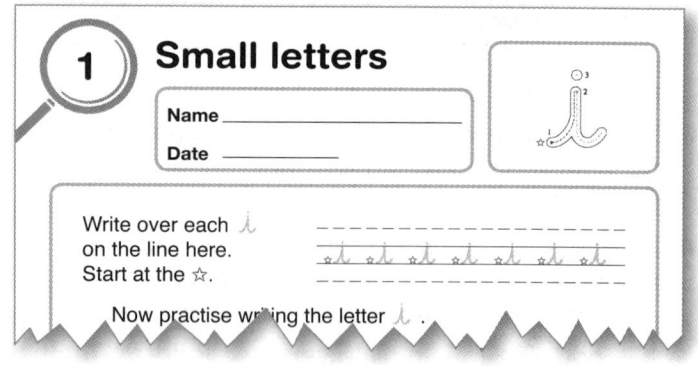

Book 1B: Year 1/P2 (Terms 2 and 3)

To provide extra practice in the transition from precursive to cursive letters, an extra book has been included at this stage. In this book, upper case letters and lower case letters are reinforced through some of the main rime patterns that will be used for spelling. In this way the development of a cursive hand is linked to the introduction of spelling patterns.

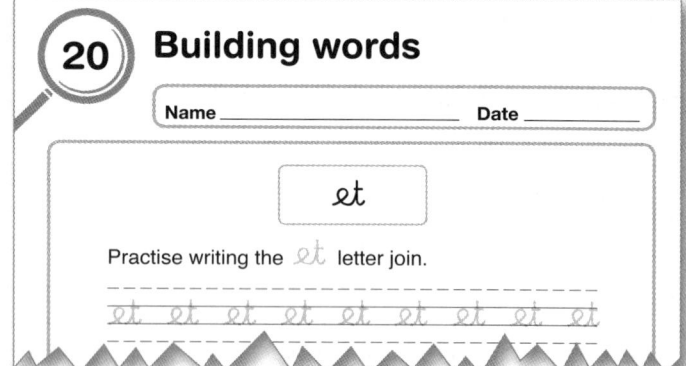

Book 2: Year 2/P3

This book continues the development of linking handwriting to spelling, introducing joins through the main onset groups and blends and the high-frequency words required to be learned and practised by the end of the Infant stage.

Junior Stage

Book 3: Year 3/P4

This book reinforces the handwriting style already learned, through sentences, spelling patterns and simple tongue-twisters and rhymes. During this book, children are encouraged to attempt writing with their eyes closed to help fix the pattern of movements in the mind. (It may be helpful if teachers show children how to place their pencil or pen on the writing line before closing their eyes!)

Through this book, children are introduced to the idea of collating a handwriting folder. Some tasks will need to be completed on another sheet of paper. This book also contains ideas for exemplar material to be retained by children in their handwriting folder.

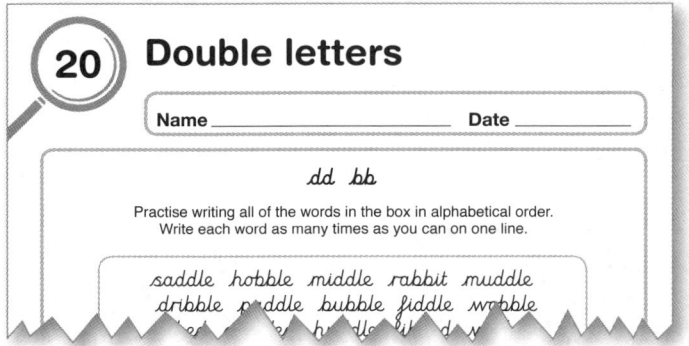

Book 4: Year 4/P5

At this stage, children are encouraged to examine different handwriting purposes and styles. This book also includes settings in which print letters may be appropriate both in upper case and lower case forms.

Links with common spelling rules and patterns and common high and medium-frequency vocabulary are continued. This book also introduces practice in writing at speed.

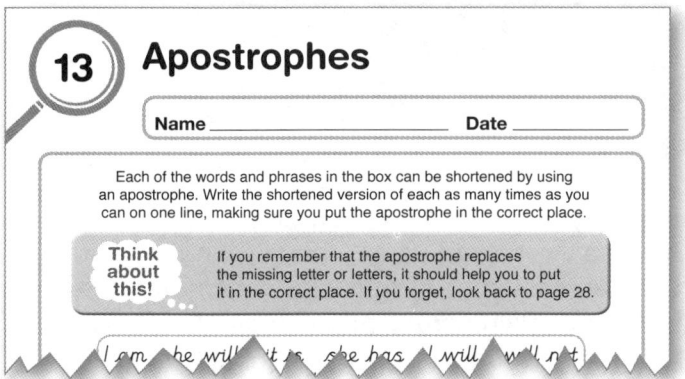

Book 5: Year 5/P6

Throughout this book, children explore different contexts in which a well-formed handwriting style plays an important part. They are asked to use both print and joined styles to transform material from a range of curricula and everyday situations for presentation to others. By this stage, children will be developing at least three handwriting styles:

● A neat, 'best' form for presentational work that may be produced slowly and with care. This style may be part of a 'school style'.

● A speedier and sometimes less neat form for, e.g. making personal notes or copying work to be presented later. It is perfectly reasonable that some children using this style may begin to 'personalise' their writing. They may begin to add loops or serifs, adopt alternative letterforms and link upper case letters to lower case letters – as many adults do. They may also experiment with a unique signature at the foot of their work. This personalisation should be encouraged as long as it fits the criteria of being clear, fluent, legible and fast.

● A clear, well-formed print style for labels, notices, captions etc. demonstrating judgement about style, size, and spatial awareness of the room available.

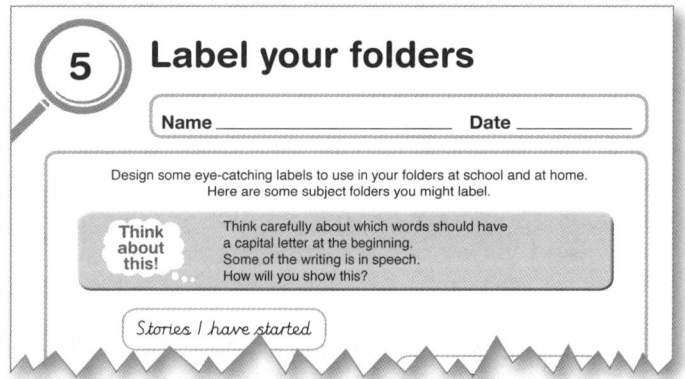

Book 6: Year 6/P7

This book extends children's mastery of the three forms of handwriting listed in the Book 5 entry on this page. Children are encouraged, through a variety of traditional calligraphy and modern presentational tasks, to develop a style that is personal and unique to themselves. (The relationship between hand-crafted and computer-aided design is extended.)

Points to remember when teaching handwriting

Seating

The seating of children for handwriting lessons is particularly important. For this reason, some teachers prefer to specify a 'handwriting table', where the light is particularly good and shines from the side or back of the children.

Many children find it more comfortable to slant their work to the side, away from their writing hand, so that they can clearly see what they are writing. For this reason, they may need more room for handwriting practice than may normally be available.

Left-handed children will need to be seated at the left-hand side of the table or desk. These children might also need a cushion or pad to provide extra height and may often benefit from a sloping surface, which might be provided by using a ring-binder file, on which to rest their paper.

Pencil/pen control

The pencil or pen should be gripped loosely between the first finger and thumb, using the second finger as a rest. The non-writing hand should be used to support and guide the paper. Many children do not learn this automatically, and it may need to be specifically taught.

Children may, even at a very early age, have learned an inappropriate grip. In some cases the hand may curl right over the pencil or pen, making their writing look extremely awkward. Teachers need to make several judgements before intervening to alter such a grip:

- If the child suffers from even a minor manual difficulty, the grip used may be the most comfortable to them.

- If their handwriting is clear, fluent, reasonably legible (to themselves and other children!) and reasonably fast, attempting to change their grip may do more harm than good. These children would benefit from the same practice in patterning and fluency as those with cramped or jerky hand movements. Tips on detecting and correcting difficulties can be found on pp.13–15 of the Teacher notes for Books 3 and 4.

- If altering the grip is the only solution, these children may benefit from recapping of earlier units in the programme as homework practice or in SEN support sessions, to help them relearn the correct movements.

Setting up a special handwriting table makes it easier to make pencil grips or triangular-shaped pencils or pens available for those children who find them more comfortable to use. Several suppliers make triangular-shaped pencils, which children may find more comfortable than a pencil grip.

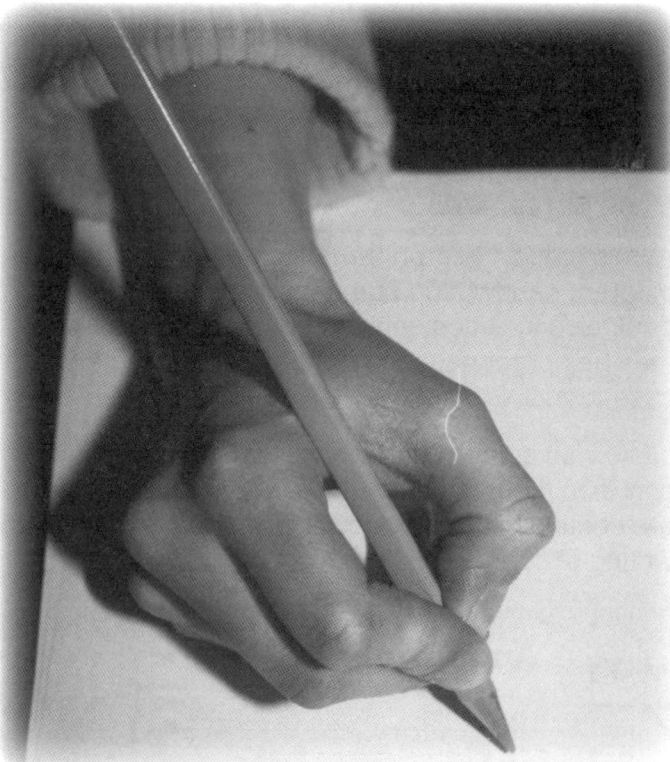

If the layout of the classroom precludes or hinders the setting-up of a handwriting table, children should be taught where their particular handwriting aids are kept and trained to find them for themselves before beginning their Handwriting lesson. Information about these implements and aids should also be made readily available to all staff members.

Materials and resources

School staff members, through their policy, may have personal preferences about whether pencil or pen should be used for 'best' handwriting. A range of implements and materials, however, should be made available to enable children to begin to make judgements and choices about what is most appropriate for a specific task. For example, children presenting shape poetry might choose to use 'jumbo' crayons or an italic pen to create a dramatic effect.

Some of the items that might be included in a resource box for handwriting are listed on this page.

Detailed notes on some of these resources may be found on pp.11–12 of the Teacher notes in Books 1A–2.

Pencils and pens

- A range of pencils of differing hardness. They should be of reasonable length and sharpened, but not to the point where they snap on use.
- Cartridge or fountain pens (because a pen, like a cook's knife, becomes shaped to a particular hand).
- Rollerball, felt-tip and fibre-tip pens.
- Coloured fibre-tip pens for artistic work.
- Italic pens (for all to try and for those who choose to create particular effects).

Paper

- Plenty of 'first draft' paper.
- Ruled guideline sheets for placing under work.
- Good-quality cartridge paper of different colours for 'best' presentation work. Teachers may wish to reserve this for special work.
- Different-sized paper, e.g. A4, A5, letter-size for notes and letters.
- Thin card, some of which might be pre-folded.
- Different-shaped papers and cards for poetry etc.
- Pre-decorated borders and mounts (preferably made in advance by the children).

Peripherals

- Triangular-shaped pencils and a selection of pencil grips.
- Ring-binder files or wedge-shaped blocks on which to rest and slant work.
- Rulers for measuring and to help keep lines straight.
- Cushions or seat pads to give extra height.

The writing environment

These items might be on display in the writing area:

- A sample sheet showing computer fonts available.
- Examples of computer-generated 'word art'.
- The alphabet in upper case and lower case letters.
- Exemplar material completed by children.
- Reminder notices, e.g. 'Don't forget the finger space!'

Organisation and timing of lessons

By this stage in the programme, many children will be gaining confidence in a joined handwriting style and may complete much of their work independent of direct support. Books 3 and 4, however, still contain material on specific letter joins, spelling patterns and other material that will link to aspects of Literacy work.

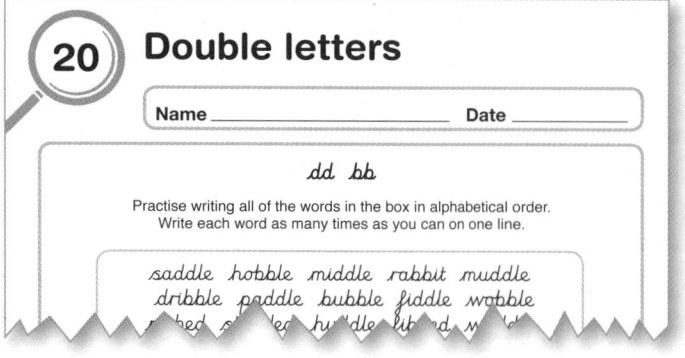

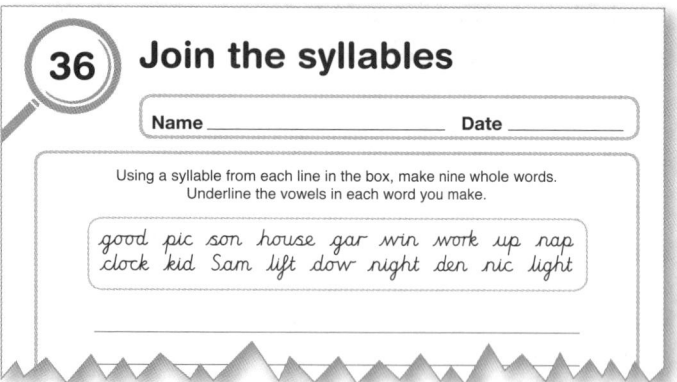

Some teachers will wish to continue the practice of a regular handwriting lesson (see p.13 of the Teacher notes in Books 1A-2). Even where teachers feel that they can integrate the teaching of handwriting with other aspects of Literacy, they will need to provide:

- Some opportunity within whole-class shared sessions, perhaps within the Literacy lesson, to demonstrate new points, emphasise the three different handwriting styles (see p.9), highlight class errors, or to link the purposes of handwriting to other work.

- Regular guided group sessions, preferably at least once a week/fortnight, in particular to observe specific children and to detect possible errors before they become entrenched.

- Support for children with specific handwriting difficulties.

- Daily opportunity for independent practice, possibly as homework.

NB: More detailed notes on the handwriting lesson, Practice and Reinforcement and Assessment may be found in the Teacher Notes for Books 1A-2.

Handwriting and the use of ICT

It is now becoming possible to use a cursive font to demonstrate joined handwriting on computer. This may enable teachers to produce supplementary material for children to practise or examples of texts used for other aspects of the literacy lesson. Books 3–6 also suggest activities that may be completed using a computer keyboard. These are specifically intended to focus on layout, design and presentational skills.

Collins Primary Focus: Handwriting, in conjunction with handwriting computer software, aims to link manual handwriting with computer-generated handwriting from the earliest stages. Software may be used to create extra worksheets for practice and reinforcement. Children may also be able to print out their stories, poems and non-fiction writing using handwriting software that features a cursive style.

Detecting and correcting difficulties

How many left-handers are there in your class? Did you know that left-handers often find it difficult to write with a hard pencil? They may grip more tightly and press down harder on the paper. A softer lead pencil may be easier for them to use.

Are all the left-handers in your class able to sit at the left-hand side of a desk for the handwriting session? Are their seats high enough? Are they able to slant and slope their work? Do they use their right hand to steady the paper? Checking these points early can save a great deal of time later remedying poor habits.

Some children with mild dyspraxia may have jerky or shaky hand movements and will never achieve a style of handwriting that looks 'regular'. But they may still achieve a comfortable and legible handwriting style that can be produced at speed.

Many children find triangular-shaped pencils more comfortable to hold and use than a separate pencil grip. Thus it is important to have a range of different writing implements available for the handwriting lesson.

There is a very strong link between handwriting and spelling. People often find that they can write something familiar, e.g. their signature, in a better hand if they write with their eyes closed. When children are memorising a particular spelling pattern, writing the words in a joined hand with their eyes closed may help to fix the pattern in their memory. This may be of particular value to SpLD (dyslexic) children, who need strong reinforcement of the patterns within language.

Just as many people have a special 'telephone voice', so they also often have more than one standard of handwriting. Children should not be expected to achieve the most careful standard for everyday writing. 'Best' handwriting should be considered for use during the publishing stage of writing, particularly if the writing is for presentation to others.

Producing careful handwriting may be physically demanding for many children. In the early stages of learning to join letters, children should be given plenty of time and opportunity to rest their hands. As they become more fluent, short speed tasks in which fluency and legibility take precedence over style may help to prepare them for timed writing tasks or assessment.

SpLD children may, under certain circumstances, be assigned a scribe for examination work. It is helpful if they can learn to use a computer keyboard to translate their thoughts and ideas into a legible script. Handwriting software may enable them to do so.

Many teachers deplore the use of ballpoint pens for handwriting, but felt-tip and fibre-tip pens or gel writers can help children with handwriting difficulties to produce a neater hand.

Teachers may have differing views about how handwriting should be marked. It is important that all staff members agree on a policy for marking. Often they will agree to assess only work used for publication or presentation.

All teachers must be able to teach handwriting, rather than simply exhort children to improve. Difficulty with handwriting can disrupt flow of thought, and speed and organisation of writing. Teachers should aim to diagnose and correct handwriting difficulties as early as possible.

Inappropriate habits are easily acquired but not so easily remedied. Teachers should take regular opportunities to circulate among children as they practise, to observe and spot potential difficulties. Points to watch for are:

● Use of the non-writing hand to steady and support paper.
● Left-handers need to hold the pencil/pen higher in order to see their own writing.
● Copy writing: many children find it difficult to copy from the class board and may need copy placed close to their work.
● Pencil: is it of reasonable length and well-sharpened; pen: does it function well?

Tips to solve handwriting problems

These problems should only be corrected if they interfere with the speed, fluency or legibility of children's handwriting.

Encourage children to vocalise movements as they make them, particularly when they are learning to make joins. This will help to fix the pattern in their memory.

Repeating a spelling or handwriting pattern will help to fix the pattern in the child's kinaesthetic memory.

Too small writing

This may signal one of several difficulties. The child may be attempting to hide a lack of confidence in spelling knowledge, confusion about correct letter formation or general poor self-esteem and a fear of making mistakes. If it occurs for none of these reasons, it may sometimes signal a deeper emotional problem.

Try this!
- Encourage the child to take a more relaxed hold of their pencil or pen.
- Include tasks in which the aim is to write faster – writing almost always increases in size as a child writes faster.
- Use practice of handwriting patterns to relax the child's hold of the pencil or pen and thus achieve easier movements.

Too large writing

This may signal poor hand control, lack of understanding of the reason for guidelines or a lack of care.

Try this!
- Provide a light pencil line above and below the main baseline and encourage the child to touch but not go over the lines.
- Practise handwriting patterns that reach the pencil line.

- Practise short words with ascenders that must touch but not go above the line, e.g. ball, hold, old, sold.
- Reduce the spacing of the lines as the child's handwriting improves.

Poor letter alignment in relation to baseline

Try this!
- Give young pupils a piece of card with thick black horizontal lines ruled on it to use as guidelines.
- Work with plastic or wooden letters, asking the child to place them on a ruled line to make words. (Descenders should go below the line.)
- Practise handwriting patterns, taking care to touch the baseline.
- Write short words that have both ascenders and descenders, e.g. baby, early, yard, yell, fell, tell, hat, bat, dog, frog, jog.

Ascenders/descenders not clearly defined

Try this!
- Provide a pencil guideline at the height of the ascenders or at the depth of the descenders. It may be useful at first to space this line slightly higher than normal, to encourage the child to exaggerate the ascenders. As the child's handwriting improves, the guideline may be lowered to normal height.
- Practise using short words containing both baseline letters and ascenders, e.g. ball, wall, tall, call, blue, black, blob.

Ascenders not parallel

Ascenders go in all directions and give writing a very untidy look.

Try this!
- Ensure that the child knows what 'parallel' means.
- Practise the joined 'l' handwriting pattern – concentrate on keeping it parallel.
- Practise writing short words with several single or double ascenders, e.g. little, hall, ball, muddle, dribble, elephant.

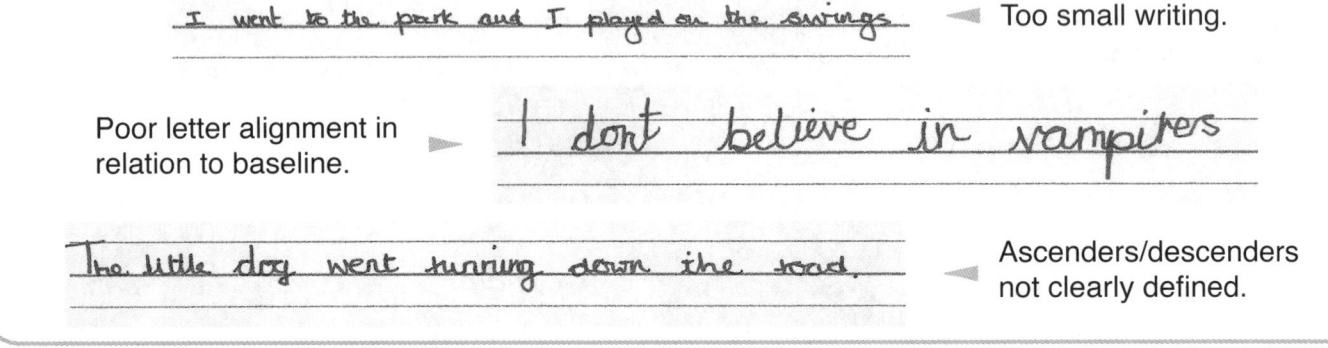

I went to the park and I played on the swings ◄ Too small writing.

Poor letter alignment in relation to baseline. ► I dont believe in vampires

The little dog went running down the road. ◄ Ascenders/descenders not clearly defined.

Too slow handwriting

Try this!

- Explain the need for the two styles of handwriting:
  - Stylish, good quality, neat handwriting for copy writing, presentation etc. This may take longer and should be produced with care.
  - Faster writing for personal notes, unpublished work etc. This may be less neat and need only be legible to the writer.
- Assign some speed writing tasks in which the child works against the clock or a timer. Accompany these tasks with an instruction, e.g. 'See how many words you can write in one minute.'
- Count and record.
- Repeat the practice and encourage the child to work against their own personal 'best' score. The child or their partner should keep a record.

Speed writing is also of help to those children who leave too large a space between words. This may be caused by the child fearing that they do not have enough subject matter to write about and therefore spreading out a little writing to look as if it is more than it actually is. Another activity to correct this is to dictate a passage that children must write as it is read. The need to get words down in time can often remedy the problem of too large spaces.

If children leave too little space, reverse the process, slowing down their writing to give them time to place a finger after each word. Leaving a 'finger space' between words is one thing many of us remember from our handwriting lessons!

Cramped and 'jerky' movements (where the child displays no other evidence of dyspraxia)

Try this!

- Practise handwriting patterns or words with a similar onset, rime or spelling pattern.
- Encourage the child to vocalise the movement involved: 'Up and down and round' etc. Then encourage the child to write the same words with their eyes closed and to 'feel' the pattern as they write.
- For those with severe difficulty, write with finger-paint or a dry finger on paper or in sand; or use a leadless pencil.
- After practice, one 'special' task may be to form the pattern with a glue-pen and then shake sand or glitter over it to produce a sparkly pattern.

Too fast ('careless') writing

Ensure that this is not the result of motor or learning difficulties.

Try this!

- Give practice in patterning and finger-writing (as for those displaying slow and 'jerky' handwriting).
- Ensure an understanding of the two handwriting styles.
- Ask the child to copy a short verse or sentence, first in 'ordinary' writing and then in 'best' writing. Ask them to make the two styles look as different as possible. This slows down the writer. Discuss differences with the child.
- Provide practice in patterns and word patterns using the child's 'best' handwriting style. Ensure that the child has plenty of time to complete the tasks.

▼ 'Note'-writing done at speed.

If plants do not get enough light, they grow very tall and

▼ Too large spaces between words.

There   are   Several   different

▼ 'Best' handwriting.

The dog fetched the bone to the boy.

Book 4

Year 4/P5 – Presentational writing

At this stage, children should be encouraged to examine different handwriting purposes and styles, looking at different fonts and alternative letter shapes.

This book also includes settings in which print letters may be appropriate both in upper case and lower case forms. Children are encouraged from this stage to develop a personal style that may differ in some of the letterforms from the style taught earlier.

Children are encouraged to extend their ideas about the purposes for which clear and careful handwriting plays a part. They are also encouraged to undertake some tasks at speed to see how well they can sustain their handwriting style under pressure.

Although some children will continue to need the support of guided group or individual work, most will now be able to work independently from this and subsequent books in the programme. For this reason, no specific pages have been marked 👥. Teachers may still wish, however, to use pages for demonstration purposes.

Practice of key vocabulary is continued using medium-frequency words. Book 4 also provides practice of compound words and syllables. Coverage of punctuation relates to the use of the apostrophe.

Pages 17–19

These pages provide an opportunity for children to both recap on work from the previous year and to set a standard for the coming year. (Teachers may wish children to repeat the self-assessment checklist from Book 3.)

The patterns of borders and linked letters will provide material for diagnostic assessment on the part of the teacher.

Children should be encouraged to think of occasions when decorated letters, patterns or borders might enhance work that is being presented to an audience. They should also be encouraged to think in advance about the tools they may require; for example, pens or crayons with shaped nibs, ruler, protractor etc. The patterns for borders may be simple arrangements of repeated lines, curves, diamonds etc. Criteria for assessment should be awareness of using space well and keeping the size and repetition of the pattern consistent.

Pages 20–22

These pages offer revision of the important joins between letters. For some children, they may provide extra opportunity to master these joins.

Pages 24–27

These pages focus on opportunities to use 'best' handwriting when sending messages or greetings to other people. Teachers may wish to link them to particular occasions during the school year. Alternatively, children may begin a collection of suitable examples of greetings cards, postcards, letters etc. in their handwriting folder, for use as and when the need arises.

Pages 28, 30–31, 46–48, 56–57

As children become more fluent in joining complete words, the repetition of these words using a 'Look, Say, Cover, Write and Check' approach is supported by the 'feeling of a pattern or string' gained by the hand. Children should be encouraged to practise each word several times at speed during the handwriting lesson. Computer keyboard practice in typing a list of words containing the same string or pattern also helps to build up this fingertip knowledge. If, in addition, children then attempt words with their eyes closed, this fingertip awareness is strengthened. Children may also be encouraged to use this type of approach when correcting errors in their other handwriting.

Pages 32–35, 37–39

The breaking of words into chunks or syllables for spelling is something that many children find very difficult. These pages offer reinforcement, initially in the notion of compound words and then in the splitting of words into their component syllables.

The remaining pages provide exemplar material for the use of differing handwriting styles for different purposes. They may, if teachers wish, be substituted or extended by tasks that relate directly to other work in the curriculum.

Page 64

A set of guidelines is included for use when teachers wish children to repeat or practise specific task pages on separate sheets of paper. Teachers may copy the page and children may write directly onto the page, or use it as a guide by placing it underneath a sheet of plain paper.

1 All about me!

Name _____ **Date** _____

Tell your friends something about yourself. Begin by writing some sentences.
Then use connectives to join your sentences together
in one paragraph.

Think about this! Since you began your last Handwriting folder, you have grown quite a bit. Think about how you have changed and what you have learned during the past year. At the end of this year, you will be able to look back to see how you have progressed.

_____

_____

_____

_____

_____

_____

_____

_____

_____

_____

_____

_____

_____

_____

How did you do? Brilliant! ☐ OK ☐ I need another try. ☐

Name _____ Date _____

Set out a title for your handwriting folder. Add your name, class and the date to the front cover. Then you might decorate the borders with patterns.

My _____
Handwriting folder

Name _____

Class _____

Date _____

How did you do? Brilliant! ☐ OK ☐ I need another try. ☐

3 Decorative patterns

Name ______________________ Date ____________

Here are some patterns that you might use to decorate your work.
Try these first and then design some patterns of your own.

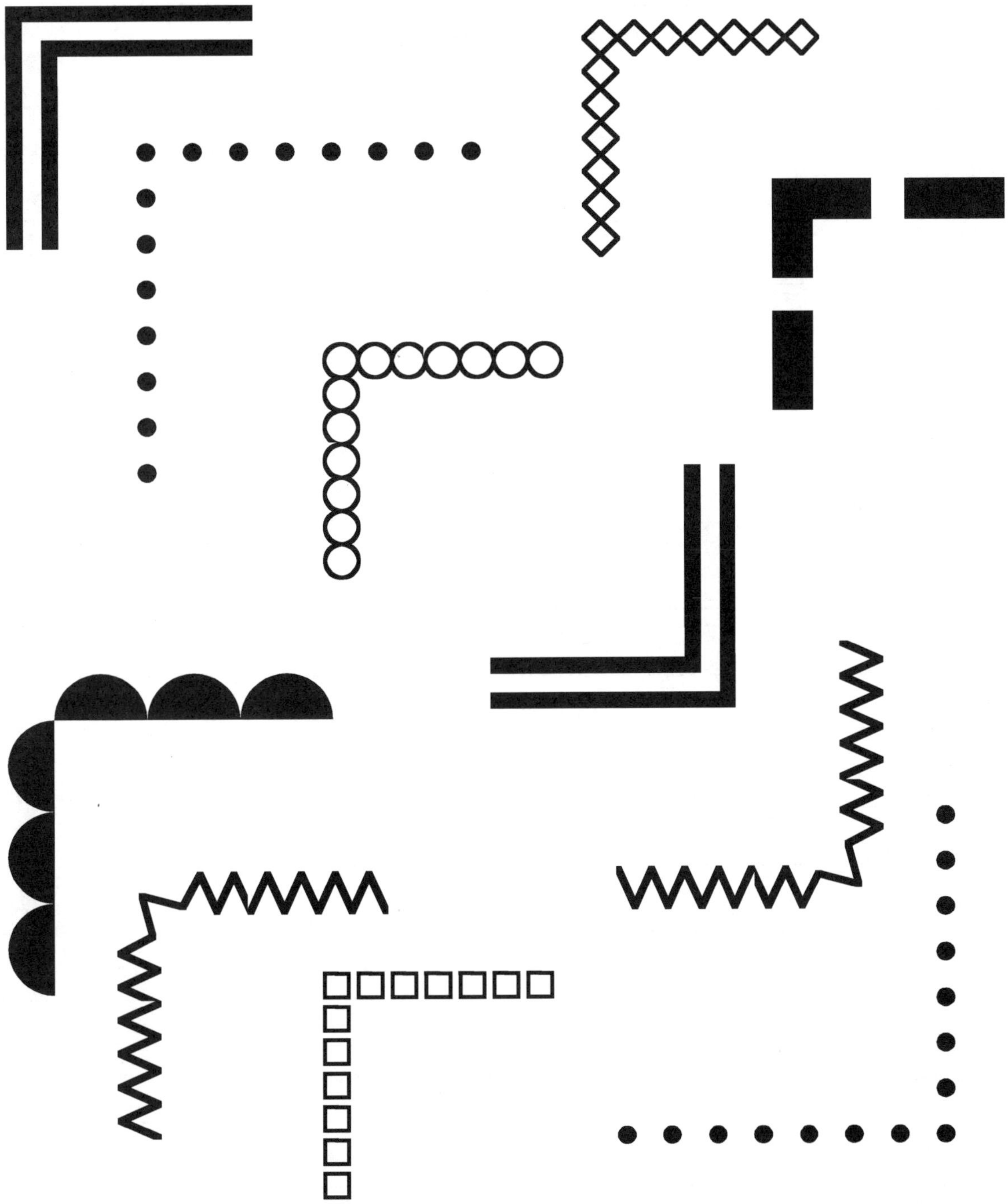

Think about this!

Repeating a pattern is a very simple way to decorate things. You might make your own bookmark or decorate your schoolbooks or homework files, but first ask your teacher for permission!
A copied poem looks very attractive with a decorated border.

Name _____ **Date** _____

ar ai ab un

Write as many words as you can think of that contain one
or more of these letter joins.

ar _____

_____

_____

_____

ai _____

_____

_____

_____

ab _____

_____

_____

_____

un _____

_____

_____

_____

How did you do? Brilliant! ☐ OK ☐ I need another try. ☐

Letter joins

Name _____ **Date** _____

ou   ri   wi   it

Write as many words as you can think of that contain one
or more of these letter joins.

ou _____

_____

_____

_____

ri _____

_____

_____

_____

wi _____

_____

_____

_____

it _____

_____

_____

_____

How did you do?   Brilliant! ☐   OK ☐   I need another try. ☐

Name _____ Date _____

al *ul* *ot* *wh*

Write as many words as you can think of that contain one
or more of these letter joins.

al _____

_____

_____

_____

ul _____

_____

_____

_____

ot _____

_____

_____

_____

wh _____

_____

_____

_____

**How did
you do?**   Brilliant! ☐   OK ☐   I need another try. ☐

A verse for a Valentine card

Name _____ Date _____

Write this well-known verse. Then you may like to write
a version of your own.

Roses are red,
Violets are blue,
Sugar is sweet
And so are You!

_____

_____

_____

_____

_____

_____

Think about this! People like to send and receive Valentine cards.
The cards should be anonymous, so people have
to guess who they are from.
Sometimes, the verses are funny and even cheeky.
Make a Valentine card for someone you like.

How did you do? Brilliant! ☐   OK ☐   I need another try. ☐

8 Design a card

Design a card to celebrate a special occasion. Choose one of the occasions listed below or one of your own. Decorate the borders.

Happy Birthday!   Congratulations!
Happy Anniversary   Merry Christmas
Happy New Year   Good Luck!

How did you do?   Brilliant! ☐   OK ☐   I need another try. ☐

Address an envelope

Name _____ **Date** _____

Now set out the address of the person you will send your card to.
You might use the address of one of your friends or make one up.

Think about this!

Remember to use the correct punctuation in the address.
Be especially careful with abbreviations.
Don't forget the postcode!

How did you do?   Brilliant! ☐   OK ☐   I need another try. ☐

Name _____ **Date** _____

Turn this page on its side and write a postcard to a friend describing a holiday.
Don't forget to mention the weather!

To:

How did you do? Brilliant! ☐ OK ☐ I need another try. ☐

Name _____ **Date** _____

Here are some terms you might hear during a weather forecast.
Copy them out in your best handwriting.

> a bracing breeze   occasional showers
> good clear spells   heavy cloud cover
> dry and sunny   a slight flurry of snow
> long periods of sunshine
> dense mist over high ground   a sharp frost
> some danger of flooding blizzard conditions

_____

_____

_____

_____

_____

_____

_____

_____

_____

_____

_____

_____

_____

_____

How did you do? Brilliant! ☐   OK ☐   I need another try. ☐

Some words you should know

Name _____ **Date** _____

Write the words in the box in alphabetical order. Then practise reading and spelling them with your partner.

Think about this!

To help you remember these words, practise writing each one at least five times.
Remember to Look, Say, Cover, Write and Check!
Try not to lift your pencil off the paper until you have finished a whole word.
When you have finished, place your pencil on the line and try writing each word again with your eyes closed.

> coming can't asked do not doesn't
> began don't did not cannot didn't
> does not brought

_____

_____

_____

_____

_____

_____

_____

_____

_____

_____

How did you do? Brilliant! ☐ OK ☐ I need another try. ☐

Apostrophes

Name _____ Date _____

Each of the words and phrases in the box can be shortened by using an apostrophe. Write the shortened version of each as many times as you can on one line, making sure you put the apostrophe in the correct place.

Think about this!

If you remember that the apostrophe replaces the missing letter or letters, it should help you to put it in the correct place. If you forget, look back to page 28.

I am   he will   it is   she has   I will   will not
do not   shall not   did not   would not

_____

_____

_____

_____

_____

_____

_____

_____

_____

_____

_____

_____

_____

How did you do?   Brilliant! ▢   OK ▢   I need another try. ▢

Some words you should know

Write the words in the box in alphabetical order. Then practise reading and spelling them with your partner.

Think about this!

To help you remember these words, practise writing each one at least five times.
Remember to Look, Say, Cover, Write and Check!
Try not to lift your pencil off the paper until you have finished a whole word.
When you have finished, place your pencil on the line and try writing each word again with your eyes closed.

stopped I'm gone opened heard started leave know show I am jumped knew

_____

_____

_____

_____

_____

_____

_____

_____

_____

_____

_____

How did you do?   Brilliant! ☐   OK ☐   I need another try. ☐

Some words you should know

Name _____ Date _____

Write the words in the box in alphabetical order. Then practise reading and spelling them with your partner.

Think about this!

To help you remember these words, practise writing each one at least five times.
Remember to Look, Say, Cover, Write and Check!
Try not to lift your pencil off the paper until you have finished a whole word.
When you have finished, place your pencil on the line and try writing each word again with your eyes closed.

> *tries woken think watch turned used write woke thought walked told*

_____

_____

_____

_____

_____

_____

_____

_____

_____

_____

_____

How did you do?   Brilliant! ☐   OK ☐   I need another try. ☐

Compound words

Make ten compound words by joining a word from the first box
with a word from the second box.

Think about this!

Compound words are made up of shorter words.
Each of the compound words on this page has two parts,
e.g. walk + about = walkabout.
You might make some matching cards for younger
children, writing each part of a compound word on
one side of a jigsaw piece and illustrating it on the other.

> snow play round bath corn sun moon
> star rain sea

> ground fish about man light flake coat
> flower room side

_____

_____

_____

_____

_____

_____

_____

_____

_____

_____

How did you do? Brilliant! ☐   OK ☐   I need another try. ☐

www.collinseducation.com © HarperCollins*Publishers* Limited 2011

Name _____ Date _____

Add the prefix "al" to each of the words in the box, then write each
new compound word as many times as you can on one line.
Can you think of any more compound words featuring the "al" prefix?

Think about this!

Each of the new compound words has two parts.
Draw a line between the syllables in each word.
You might make some matching cards for younger
children, writing each part of a compound word on one
side of a jigsaw piece and illustrating it on the other.

most though ready so arm together cove
low right ways as tar arming

_____

_____

_____

_____

_____

_____

_____

_____

_____

_____

How did you do? Brilliant! ☐ OK ☐ I need another try. ☐

Compound words

Name _____ Date _____

Make eight compound words by joining a word from
the first box with a word from the second box and a word
from the third box.

Think about this! Compound words are made up of shorter words. Each of the compound words on this page has three parts, e.g. games + man + ship = gamesmanship. You might make some matching cards for younger children, writing each part of a compound word on one side of a jigsaw piece.

> in up here what in who here whom

> to in side so so so side so

> ever fore ever far ever after down out

_____

_____

_____

_____

_____

_____

_____

_____

How did you do? Brilliant! ☐ OK ☐ I need another try. ☐

Compound words

Name _____ **Date** _____

Use the words in the box to help you make as many two-part compound words as you can. Each word from the box can be used as the first part or the second part of different compound words. Write each new word as many times as you can on one line.

Think about this! Underline the vowels and draw a line between the syllables in each of your new compound words. You might make some matching cards for younger children, writing each part of a compound word on one side of a jigsaw piece and illustrating it on the other.

> *after day rain night in out storm down snow under suit sea green*

_____

_____

_____

_____

_____

_____

_____

_____

_____

_____

_____

How did you do? Brilliant! ☐ OK ☐ I need another try. ☐

Handwriting check 1:
"The Iron Man"

Name _____ Date _____

Here is the beginning of a story you may know. Write it in your best handwriting. You may want to draw your own picture of the Iron Man.

Think about this!

Ted Hughes was a famous poet who also wrote stories for children. He set out his writing almost like a poem. As you write, think about the punctuation. How do the commas help you to read the story aloud?

The Iron Man came to the top of the cliff.
How far had he walked? Nobody knows.
How was he made? Nobody knows.
Taller than a house, the Iron Man stood
at the top of the cliff, on the very brink,
in the darkness.
The wind sang through his iron fingers.
His great iron head, shaped like a dustbin
but as big as a bedroom, slowly turned to the
right, slowly turned to the left.
His iron ears turned, this way, that way.
He was hearing the sea.
His eyes, like headlamps, glowed white, then
red, then infra-red, searching the sea.
Never before had the Iron Man seen the sea.

Ted Hughes

21 Syllables

Write the two-syllable words in the box in alphabetical order.
Underline all of the vowels in each word, then add a line to show
where each syllable break is.

Think about this! You might make a set of syllable jigsaws for younger children, as you did with the compound words on pages 32–35.

> patter flipper shopper hummer finger
> dragon thunder monkey flower shadow
> cover lightning tiger

How did you do? Brilliant! ☐ OK ☐ I need another try. ☐

22 Syllables

Name _____ Date _____

Write the three-syllable words in the box in alphabetical order.
Underline all of the vowels in each word, then add a line to show
where each syllable break is.

Think about this! You might make a set of syllable jigsaws for younger children, as you did with the compound words on pages 32–35.

telephone butterfly supervise irrigate bicycle
mystify holiday educate skeleton opening
calendar motorway accident

_____

_____

_____

_____

_____

_____

_____

_____

_____

_____

_____

_____

How did you do? Brilliant! ☐ OK ☐ I need another try. ☐

Name _____ Date _____

Write the multi-syllable words in the box in alphabetical order.
Underline all of the vowels in each word, then add a line to show
where each syllable break is.

Think about this! You might make a set of syllable jigsaws for younger children, as you did with the compound words on pages 32–35.

> meteorology hippopotamus explanation
> rhinoceros onomatopoeia vaccination
> astronomy environment tonsillectomy
> terrestrial binoculars artificial identification

_____

_____

_____

_____

_____

_____

_____

_____

_____

_____

_____

How did you do? Brilliant! ☐ OK ☐ I need another try. ☐

Name _____ Date _____

A kenning describes something without using its name. Think about which creatures are described by kennings in this poem. Write this poem in your best handwriting. You might decorate it with illustrations of all the creatures mentioned.

Think about this! Look carefully at each line to see which has a comma and which a full stop.
Who do you think "Two-boots" is?

Two-boots in the forest walks,
Pushing through the bracken stalks.

Vanishing like a puff of smoke,
Nimbletail flies up the oak.

Long ears helter-skelter shoots
Into his house among the roots.

At work upon the highest bark,
Tapperbill knocks off to hark.

Painted-wings through sun and shade
Flounces off along the glade.

Not a creature lingers by,
When clumping Two-boots comes to pry.

James Reeves

Pronunciation

Name _____ **Date** _____

"ph" says "f"

In Greek, an "f" sound is often made by using "ph". Write the words in the box in alphabetical order, then practise reading them aloud with your partner.

> physical phew pharmacist photocopy
> pheasant phase phoneme phrase phonecard
> phantom photograph phobia physics

_____

_____

_____

_____

_____

_____

_____

_____

_____

_____

_____

_____

How did you do? Brilliant! ☐   OK ☐   I need another try. ☐

Name _____ Date _____

Write each of the following sentences in your best handwriting.

Please do not walk on the grass.

_____

_____

_____

Please keep your dog on a lead.

_____

_____

_____

Please take your litter home with you.

_____

_____

_____

Please drive carefully.

_____

_____

_____

How did you do? Brilliant! ☐ OK ☐ I need another try. ☐

www.collinseducation.com © HarperCollins*Publishers* Limited 2011

"Thank-you" sentences

Name _____ Date _____

Write each of the following sentences in your best handwriting.

Thank you for coming.

_____

_____

_____

Thank you for inviting me.

_____

_____

_____

Thank you for not smoking.

_____

_____

_____

Thank you for keeping our playground tidy.

_____

_____

_____

How did you do? Brilliant! ☐ OK ☐ I need another try. ☐

"Do" and "Don't" sentences

Name _____ **Date** _____

Write each of the following sentences in your best handwriting.

Do keep your coats tidy.

_____

_____

_____

Do remember to say "Please" and "Thank you".

_____

_____

_____

Don't run in the corridors.

_____

_____

_____

Don't fight in the playground.

_____

_____

_____

How did you do? Brilliant! ☐   OK ☐   I need another try. ☐

Handwriting check 3:
Proverbs

Name _____ **Date** _____

Write each of the following proverbs in your best handwriting.

A stitch in time saves nine.

_____

_____

_____

Too many cooks spoil the broth.

_____

_____

_____

A fool and his money are soon parted.

_____

_____

_____

A watched pot never boils.

_____

_____

_____

How did you do?   Brilliant! ☐   OK ☐   I need another try. ☐

Name _____ Date _____

Write the words in the box in alphabetical order. Then practise reading and spelling them with your partner.

Think about this! ...

To help you remember these words, practise writing each one at least five times.
Remember to Look, Say, Cover, Write and Check!
Try not to lift your pencil off the paper until you have finished a whole word.
When you have finished, place your pencil on the line and try writing each word again with your eyes closed.

> half morning during almost first better
> much every always before any

_____

_____

_____

_____

_____

_____

_____

_____

_____

How did you do? Brilliant! ☐   OK ☐   I need another try. ☐

Some words you should know

Name _____ Date _____

Write the words in the box in alphabetical order. Then practise reading and spelling them with your partner.

Think about this!

To help you remember these words, practise writing each one at least five times.
Remember to Look, Say, Cover, Write and Check!
Try not to lift your pencil off the paper until you have finished a whole word.
When you have finished, place your pencil on the line and try writing each word again with your eyes closed.

only font number colon second hyphen
never connective often clause comma

_____

_____

_____

_____

_____

_____

_____

_____

_____

_____

_____

How did you do?   Brilliant! ☐   OK ☐   I need another try. ☐

Some words you should know

Name _____ **Date** _____

Write the words in the box in alphabetical order. Then practise reading and spelling them with your partner.

Think about this! ...

To help you remember these words, practise writing each one at least five times.
Remember to Look, Say, Cover, Write and Check!
Try not to lift your pencil off the paper until you have finished a whole word.
When you have finished, place your pencil on the line and try writing each word again with your eyes closed.

> young today suddenly until sometimes
> year whole upon still those while

_____

_____

_____

_____

_____

_____

_____

_____

_____

_____

How did you do?   Brilliant! ☐   OK ☐   I need another try. ☐

Name _____ **Date** _____

Write each of the following sentences in your best handwriting.

Think before you speak.

_____

_____

_____

Don't interrupt another speaker.

_____

_____

_____

Speak slowly and clearly.

_____

_____

_____

Listen carefully to the opinions of others.

_____

_____

_____

How did you do? Brilliant! ☐ OK ☐ I need another try. ☐

Name _____ Date _____

"f" into "ves"

Write the words in the box in their plural form.
Remember to change each word ending.

> scarf life dwarf wife knife self leaf
> loaf wolf calf elf sheaf hoof

_____

_____

_____

_____

_____

_____

_____

_____

_____

_____

_____

How did you do? Brilliant! ☐ OK ☐ I need another try. ☐

Handwriting check 4:
Proverbs

Name _____ Date _____

Write each of the following proverbs in your best handwriting.

Red sky at night, shepherd's delight; red sky in the morning, shepherd's warning.

_____

_____

_____

_____

_____

One swallow does not make a summer.

_____

_____

_____

Ne'er cast a clout till May be out.

_____

_____

_____

How did you do? Brilliant! ☐   OK ☐   I need another try. ☐

Decorating letters

Name_____ Date _____

These capital letters illustrate different styles and decoration.
Draw each letter in a box in a different style and decorate them all.

B T D M S

How did you do? Brilliant! ☐ OK ☐ I need another try. ☐

Decorating letters

Name _____ **Date** _____

Decorate the two enlarged capital letters at the beginning of this prayer.

> **Think about this!**
>
> Decorated letters are often used for prayers, poems and mottoes.
> Scribes spent weeks and even years painting beautiful pictures to decorate the first capital letter on the page of a book.
> Make a bookmark and decorate it with the initials of your name.

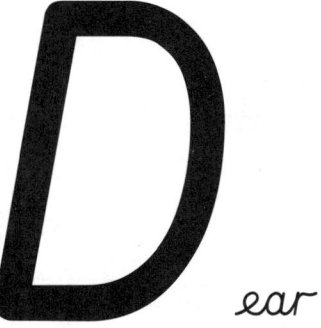

D ear

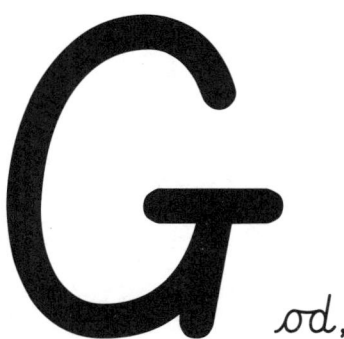

G od,

Who watches over all creatures,
Watch over me, at home and at school.

How did you do? Brilliant! ☐ OK ☐ I need another try. ☐

A speed writing test

Name _____ **Date** _____

Try writing each of these tongue-twisters as quickly as you can on separate sheets of paper. Can you keep your handwriting neat?

The quick brown fox jumps over the lazy dog.

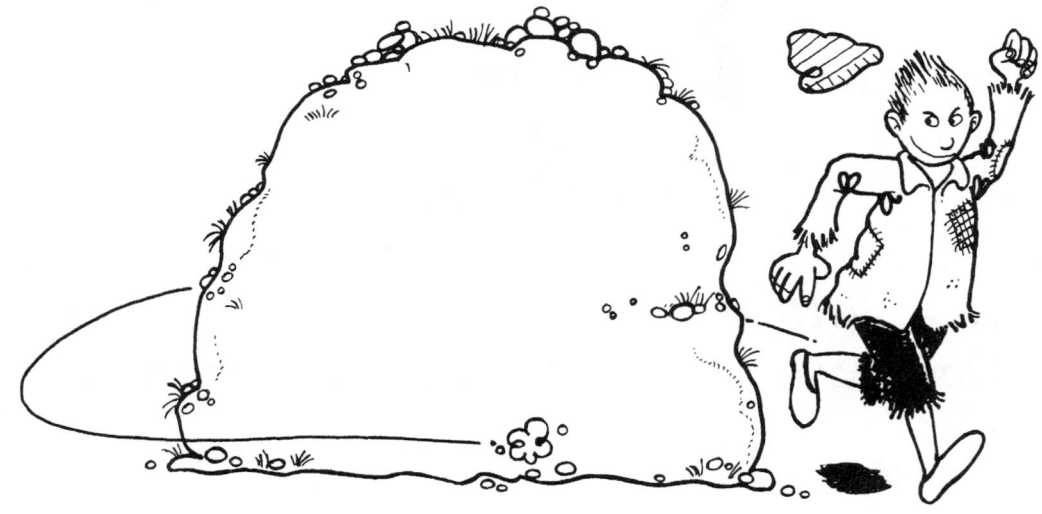

Around the rugged rock, the ragged rascal ran.

It's an apostrophe!

Name _____ **Date** _____

Which of the **its** and **it's** in the following sentences should have an apostrophe and which should not? Write the corrected sentences on another sheet of paper.

Think about this! If you can split **it's** into **it is** without destroying the sense of the sentence, it should have an apostrophe. If you can't, it shouldn't!

The cat was washing its whiskers.

The old oak tree had shed its leaves in the autumn gales.

Its a good thing I brought my umbrella.

When you think its going to be sunny, it often rains.

Some words you should know

Name _____ **Date** _____

Write the words in the box in alphabetical order. Then practise reading and spelling them with your partner.

Think about this! To help you remember these words, practise writing each one at least five times.
Remember to Look, Say, Cover, Write and Check!
Try not to lift your pencil off the paper until you have finished a whole word.
When you have finished, place your pencil on the line and try writing each word again with your eyes closed.

below following different along both across also between inside high around above

_____

_____

_____

_____

_____

_____

_____

_____

_____

_____

_____

How did you do? Brilliant! ☐ OK ☐ I need another try. ☐

Some words you should know

Name _____ Date _____

Write the words in the box in alphabetical order. Then practise reading and spelling them with your partner.

Think about this! To help you remember these words, practise writing each one at least five times.
Remember to Look, Say, Cover, Write and Check!
Try not to lift your pencil off the paper until you have finished a whole word.
When you have finished, place your pencil on the line and try writing each word again with your eyes closed.

where   other   near   together   round   outside
such   place   without   through   right   under

_____

_____

_____

_____

_____

_____

_____

_____

_____

_____

How did you do?   Brilliant! ☐   OK ☐   I need another try. ☐

Unusual epitaphs

Name _____ Date _____

Write the following unusual epitaphs found on gravestones.
You might use your research skills to find some more examples.

Stay, selfish man
And drop a tear.
Jane's little bird
Lies buried here.

Here lies what's left
Of Leslie Moore.
No Les,
No more.

Sir Vere-Burns RIP
Here lies a man who was
killed by lightning;
He died when his prospects
seemed to be brightening.
He might have cut a flash in
this world of trouble,
But the flash cut him and he
lies in the stubble.

Name _____ **Date** _____

These phrases are all used when people want to sell something.
Use them to help you write a newspaper advertisement selling an
imaginary item. Then design a poster advertising the item for sale.

Think about this!

When advertising items for sale, people often use print
instead of joined writing to highlight important words
and phrases. Sometimes they will enlarge, **highlight** or
italicise words.
Each word costs money, so think where you might use
a dash instead of a complete sentence to save space.

For Sale   one careful owner   still boxed
slightly shopsoiled   some attention needed
in perfect condition   free to a good home
can deliver   price reflects condition
good with children   would suit large family

_____

_____

_____

_____

_____

_____

_____

_____

How did you do?   Brilliant! ☐   OK ☐   I need another try. ☐

Handwriting check 5:
Proverbs

Name _____ Date _____

Write each of the following proverbs in your best handwriting.

A fair exchange is no robbery.

_____

_____

_____

A bird in the hand is worth two in the bush.

_____

_____

_____

Don't count your chickens before they are hatched.

_____

_____

_____

Don't put all your eggs in one basket.

_____

_____

_____

How did you do?   Brilliant! ☐   OK ☐   I need another try. ☐

Handwriting check 6:
"From a railway carriage"

45

Name _____ Date _____

Write this poem in your best handwriting.

Think about this!

Look carefully at all of the punctuation marks used in this poem. Why has each one been chosen? How do they help you to read the poem out loud?

Faster than fairies, faster than witches,
Bridges and houses, hedges and ditches;
And charging along like troops in a battle,
All through the meadows, the horses and cattle;
All of the sights of the hill and the plain
Fly as thick as driving rain;
And ever again, in the wink of an eye,
Painted stations whistle by.

Here is a child who clambers and scrambles,
All by himself and gathering brambles;
Here is a tramp who stands and gazes;
And there is the green for stringing the daisies!
Here is a cart run away in the road
Lumping along with man and load;
And here is a mill, and there is a river:
Each a glimpse and gone for ever!

Robert Louis Stevenson

Writing a letter

Name _____ **Date** _____

Write this letter in your best handwriting, then use it to write your own letter to show your parents or carers how well you can write.

Think about this!

Everyone has someone special to thank for helping them learn to do things well. It might be your family, teachers or friends.
You could even design your own headed notepaper and envelopes to make your letter extra special.

Dear Mum and Dad,

As you can see, I have been learning joined handwriting. I still find some letters quite hard but I am very proud of how neat it is. I thought it would be a good idea to write you a letter to say thank you for all the things you do for me. Thank you for making sure I have delicious food to eat and a cosy warm bed to go to sleep in. Thank you for taking me out on trips and for buying me a computer so that I can surf the Internet. I like all my toys and games and most of all I like watching television.

Thank you for being my Mum and Dad.

Love from

   www.collinseducation.com © HarperCollins*Publishers* Limited 2011

Handwriting check 7:
"Cargoes"

Name _____ **Date** _____

Write this poem in your best handwriting. You might want
to learn it by heart.

Think about this!

This famous poem has a very strong rhythm.
John Masefield loved the sound of words and selected
them very carefully.
Several commas in a sentence help you to slow
down when you read it. Where there are fewer commas
you can speed up when you read.

Quinquereme of Nineveh from distant Ophir
Rowing home to haven in sunny Palestine,
With a cargo of ivory,
And apes and peacocks,
Sandalwood, cedarwood, and sweet white wine.

Stately Spanish galleon coming from the Isthmus,
Dipping through the Tropics by the palm-green
shores,
With a cargo of diamonds,
Emeralds, amethysts,
Topazes, and cinnamon and gold moidores.

Dirty British coaster with a salt-caked smoke
stack
Butting through the channel in the mad March
days,
With a cargo of Tyne coal,
Road-rail, pig-lead,
Firewood, iron-ware, and cheap tin trays.

John Masefield

www.collinseducation.com © HarperCollins*Publishers* Limited 2011